FRIENDS
OF
EBER

A Reference Guide to the Living Letters
of the Hebrew Alphabet

SECOND EDITION

By

Aaron Smith
Teresa Bowen
Elizabeth R. Corley
Y.A. Butler
Daniel Cook

SCROLLS OF ZEBULON
A PUBLISHING COMPANY

Mobile, Alabama USA

Friends of Eber: A Reference Guide to the Living Letters of the Hebrew Alphabet
© 2018 by Aaron Smith, Teresa Bowen, Elizabeth R. Corley, Y.A. Butler, and Daniel Cook

For inquiries, contact:
Scrolls of Zebulon Publishing
P.O. Box 190309
Mobile, Alabama USA 36619-0939
www.scrollsofzebulon.com — info@scrollsofzebulon.com

Cover and Interior Design by Sarah Smith
Edited by Rachel L. Hall

Unless otherwise indicated, scripture is taken from Holy Bible, King James Version.

Scripture quotations marked (NIV) are taken from the Holy Bible, New International Version®, NIV®. Copyright © 1973, 1978, 1984, 2011 by Biblica, Inc.™ Used by permission of Zondervan. All rights reserved worldwide. www.zondervan.com The "NIV" and "New International Version" are trademarks registered in the United States Patent and Trademark Office by Biblica, Inc.™

Hebrew word definitions are derived from Strong's Exhaustive Concordance of the Bible, ed. James Strong (Nashville, TN: Thomas Nelson Publishers, 1977).

ISBN: 978-1-7320203-2-0

SECOND EDITION, September 2018

Amazon Print, June 2019 – Original version reads right to left. Due to Amazon regulations, this version reads left to right.

ABOUT THE AUTHORS

Aaron Smith and his wife Robbie founded The Rock of Mobile church in Mobile, Alabama in September of 1990, where he is the Senior Minister. He is founder of OPe, Open Portal Enterprises, a technology company inspired by scripture in Ezekiel chapters one and ten and Revelation chapter four. In his spare time, Aaron enjoys golf and spending time with his family that includes seven grandchildren. Aaron is the author of *Come Up Here: The Place of Our Original Intent* (2016, Scrolls of Zebulon).

Teresa Bowen is an ordained prophet at The Rock of Mobile, where she has been part of the body and ministry team for more than 25 years. Teresa has a passion to equip the heirs of the Kingdom to rise into their original intent. At home, she loves regularly sharing meals and dreams around her table with her daughters and their families. Teresa is the author of two previous books: *Zadok: The New… Old Order* (2016) and *The Fourth Wheel Story: New Creation Man* (2017), both with Scrolls of Zebulon.

Elizabeth R. Corley has studied the Hebrew letters and language for over 30 years. She received a B.S. in Computer Science from Oral Roberts University in 1985. Since 2006, she has taught at The Rock School as the K5 through second grade teacher. In 2015, she began to include lessons on the Hebrew letters in her classroom. Her personal desire is to understand Yahweh's scriptures in the original Hebrew language and equip others to know and understand the Hebrew letters. She shares her life adventures with her husband, Andy and son, Daniel.

Y.A. Butler was greatly influenced by the commitment and personal prayer life of her foreign missionary parents, Pastor Don Caleb and Brenda Crigger. Her exposure to varying cultures and languages from a young age made it easy and fun for her to take complex ideas and turn them into simple language. Her passion for the Hebrew language started in childhood and developed as she expressed herself in music and solitary worship. After serving in ministry overseas with her husband, Ray Butler, their family relocated to Mobile, Alabama. In 2004, Y.A. began a massage ministry. She believes that therapeutic massage has the power to provide a healing touch to the mystical body of Christ. Y.A. and her family have been members of the Rock of Mobile since 1995.

Daniel Cook began a journey that led him to discover secrets in the Hebrew Aleph-Beit upon moving to Mobile, Alabama in the summer of 2000. What he learned launched a whole new way of thinking, and he was never the same again. Daniel states, "As Yahweh has taught me a whole new way of thinking, he showed me how each letter also represents my relationship with Him and our journey together. My desire is for each one who reads this book to see the life that each letter speaks." He is an avid blogger on spiritual matters at TzimTzum.life, and currently teaches Tech Support for a large technologies firm. Daniel, along with his wife Michelle and daughter Lorin, have been part of the Rock of Mobile since 2003.

Second Edition Updates

New in the Second Edition of *Friends of Eber*, you'll find the addition of the Hebrew sofit letters. These are the final forms of the letters *Khaf, Mem, Nun, Pey,* and *Tsade*, used only at the end of words.

Why are these final forms important enough to bring about an update to this book? Let one of our teachers tell you, below:

> *Just as a baker pictures the kind of cake he wants to bake before he starts to mix the ingredients, or as a farmer has in mind the crop he wants before he plants the field, these final letter forms are the finishing picture of a mature son of Yahweh. They are the inward destination that we pilot towards, using the other Hebrew letters to arrive. This journey is a process which begins once you settle in your mind that "This is who and what I am."*
>
> *These letters stand taller than the rest. They are noticed. They are different. They don't blend in. They are not ashamed. They are in good standing with God and man. They are the result of a process.*
>
> *Even though they are a finishing, it is as if we have come full-circle and have discovered a new level of who we are. These end results are actually "new dots" of another dimension. The finishing is just the beginning....*

Y.A. Butler

TABLE OF CONTENTS

FRIENDS OF EBER

INTRODUCTION

The compilation of this book grew out of a time when The Spirit of The Lord first spoke to me about learning and engaging with the Hebrew letters. Over a period of three months, I had received visitations from Melchizedek, the ancient king. During that time, Melchizedek gave me revelation on the subject of the seven thunders mentioned in Revelation, chapter 10.[1] The fifth of those seven thunders was simply *Eber*. When Melchizedek spoke the name *Eber*, I was caught off guard. I knew I had read the name before, but I had not studied or become familiar with him.

Eber has been hidden in plain sight for some time now. His name is mentioned three times in Genesis 10:21-25. Eber is an amazing character. The name *Eber* means "region beyond." In a nutshell, I believe Eber rejected the order to build the tower that was later called Babel (Gen. 11). Neither he nor his family participated. They did not even touch the tower. Because of this, Yahweh preserved the Hebrew language and gave stewardship of its original letters to Eber. Actually, the word Hebrew is based upon the name Eber.

On August 25th, 2017, we who accepted the call to come Up Here were invited to be seated in Mount Zion. Mount Zion is the place of our throne rooms, and it is from where we speak. To fully engage with the great ages of peace that have now begun, we must set ourselves to learn the rules of order of Yahweh's kingdom. In addition, we must also know His language. His language is made up of twenty-three living letters. These letters are *living* in that they are created by Yahweh, and they each have individual voices and personalities.

---

1   Details on the seven thunders can be found in *Come Up Here* (Scrolls of Zebulon, 2016).

Eber, revealed to me as the steward of the living letters, has opened the door for us to come into his speaking place. There, we meet and learn the ways of his friends, who are now also our friends. These friends are the living letters. Each one is alive and desires to speak. As we engage with them, they will reveal to us the secrets, mysteries, and truths they each hold.

This book is intended to be a reference guide. It is a result of forty-six days in the fall of 2017 when I called on the people of The Rock of Mobile to engage with Eber. We spent two days focused on each of the twenty-three letters you'll find explained here. During that time, Eber revealed unique expressions of the letters to five treasured teachers in the House of The Rock of Mobile. Over a series of services, those teachers (including me, Teresa Bowen, Y.A. Butler, Daniel Cook, and Elizabeth R. Corley) shared their revelations of the letters to help deepen the understanding we had begun to develop individually. The combination of focused individual time and the group teaching sessions paved the way for the entire body to better engage with our friends, the living letters. Due to the great response to the group teaching sessions from our extended Livestream family, we decided to put together this book for all to study.

Remember, the letters are living. Let Eber speak to you about who they are and about the secrets and truths they hold. May this study inspire you to stay engaged. Let the secrets you are meant to find no longer remain hidden.

Aaron Smith

A Brief History of the Written Hebrew Letters

Artifacts show the early Semitic Hebrew alphabet was in use at least as early as the 20th through the 12th centuries B.C. The Wadi el-Hol inscriptions, found in southern Egypt, represent the oldest known inscriptions using early Semitic Hebrew.

The middle Semitic Hebrew alphabet began during the 12th century B.C. An example can be found on the Gezer Calendar, dated 900 B.C.

The late Semitic Hebrew alphabet can be found between the 4th century B.C. and the early modern era. The majority of the Dead Sea scrolls, dated from the 2nd and 1st centuries B.C., are written in the late Semitic style.

Modern Hebrew script began around the 11th century A.D. The Masoretic Leningrad Codex is the oldest known complete work of the Hebrew Bible, dated 1010 A.D.[2]

When translating Hebrew to English, there are several phonic options. This is why some Hebrew words and Hebrew letter names will have various spellings.

Elizabeth R. Corley

We recognize and use the ordinal positions of the main Modern Hebrew letters. In the place that Yahweh has called us to at this time, we do not use the gematria. We believe, as sons and daughters, He has taught us another way. As He leads us down our own unique path, He is jealous of how we individually see and hear the letters and the positions they hold. If you desire to use gematria, then let it be your word. Blessings to your path.

Aaron Smith

---

2   Additional details on the history of the Hebrew alphabet and language can be found on The Hebrew Alphabet page on The Ancient Hebrew Research Center website: http://www.Ancient-Hebrew.org.

HEBREW LETTERS AND PRONUNCIATION

Name	Early	Middle	Late	Modern	Name	Sounds
Aleph	𐤀	✝	א	א	אָלֶף	Silent letter
Beyt	𐤁	𐤁	ב	בּ	בֵּית	/B/ as in ball
				ב	בֵית	/V/ as in void – void of a dot
Gimal	⌃	𐤂	ג	ג	גִּמֶל	/G/ as in gate
Dalet	𐤃	△	ד	ד	דָּלֶת	/D/ as in door
Hey	𐤄	𐤄	ה	ה	הֵא	/H/ as in hay
Vav	Y	𐤅	ו	ו	וָו	/V/ as in vertical line; consonantal vowel
Zayin	𐤆	𐤆	ז	ז	זַיִן	/Z/ as in Zechariah
Chet	H	𐤇	ח	ח	חֵית	/Ch/ as in Bach
Tet	𐤈	𐤈	ט	ט	טֵית	/T/ as in top
Yud	𐤉	𐤉	י	י	יוֹד	/Y/ as in yes; consonantal vowel
Kaph	𐤊	𐤊	כ	כ	כָּף	/K/ as in key
				כ		/Ch/ as in Bach
Kaph Final			ך	ך		/K/ as in duck
				ך		/Ch/ as in Bach
Lamed	∠	𐤋	ל	ל	לָמֶד	/L/ as in longest letter
Mem	⋀	𐤌	מ	מ	מֵם	/M/ as in mountain
Mem Final			ם	ם		/M/ as in Abraham

Nun	↜	𐤍	ل	נ	נוּן	/N/ as in now
Nun Final			١	ן		/N/ as in amen
Samech	≢	丰	�	ס	סָמֶךְ	/C/ as in circle or /S/ as in son
Ayin	⬭	O	y	ע	עַיִן	Silent letter
Pey	�	ز	۱	פ	פֵּא	/P/ as in profile or pea
				פ	פֵ	/Ph/ as in phone
Pey Final			↳	ף		/Ph/ as in phone
Tsade	☞	ᴦ	⅄	צ	צָדִי	/Ts/ as in nuts
Tsade Final			↱	ץ		/Ts/ as in nuts
Quph	⸙	ቶ	ⴹ	ק	קוּף	/Q/ as in queen; /K/ as in king
Resh	⟋	⟨	٦	ר	רֵישׁ	/R/ as in round
Shin	∾	W	↗	שׁ	שִׁין	/Sh/ as in shine
				שׂ	שִׂין	/S/ as in sun
Tav	+	✗	ൡ	ת ת	תָּו	/T/ as in toe
Ghah	৪					

Compiled by Elizabeth R. Corley

THE FOUR BASE LETTERS OF HEBREW

In modern and late Semitic Hebrew, there are three base letters found in several of the other letters.

The first is Yud (י). It has been said that once a pen has touched the paper, the letter Yud has been written. Therefore, every Hebrew letter contains the letter Yud. If it is the mathematical dot of the Hebrew letters, then the letter Vav is the line.

The second is Vav (ו), which has been called the extended Yud. It is the straight line and can be seen in the following letters:

אבגדההזחחטלמנעצקרשת

The third is Kaph (כ), which is the curve or half circle. It can be seen in the following letters:

למפק

A fourth letter stands alone: Samech (ס). It is the circle of the letters.

Elizabeth R. Corley

{ס-כ-ו-י}

י	the seed of Yahweh's word and the all-spark of creation	*You plant the seed/letter/thought. It sparks to life as you receive it and give it place.*
ו	man as the heaven and earth connection	*You feed/ entertain it/ meditate on it. It takes root. It extends out of itself joining heaven and earth.*
כ	beholding and becoming	*It unites with your intentions and becomes your actions.*
ס	shows us Yahweh's plan and supernatural support	*It reaches maturity and now exists independently of natural support. It becomes a portal for more seeds. Like a fractal, it expands its territory and its growth is exponential.*

These letters are a blessing and a warning.
Those who have ears to hear, let them hear.
Those who have eyes to see, let them see.

Y.A. Butler and Daniel Cook

Hebrew Alphabet

אָלֶף־בֵּית עִבְרִי

ALEPH

MODERN

| EARLY | MIDDLE | LATE |

*A**leph* is the quiet strength and stillness of the inner core connecting heaven and earth.

Quiet: Aleph is one of two letters that do not have a unique sound. It takes on the vowel sounds, but it is considered a silent letter.

Strength: The Hebrew word 'eleph (אֶלֶף) means ox (Strong's H504). An ox represents a strong burden barer. The Aleph was an ox head in the early ancient Semitic/Hebrew (𐤀).

Stillness of the inner core: The hand gesture for Aleph, suggested by the Meru Foundation, points to the body's inner core.[3]

Connecting heaven and earth: Aleph is written using a Vav (ו) and two Yuds (י). The Vav is bowing in humility and the Yuds represent the earth below and the heaven above.

Aleph is used as a prefix in verbs to mean "I will." The inner core of our will needs to connect to heaven. This became a revelation to me when I was looking at a phrase that originated in Hebrew. The first word, *abara* (אברא), is "I will create." The first Aleph is the prefix "I will." The word *bara* (בָּרָא) means *create* (Strong's H1254). The second word of the phrase is *Kadavara* (כדברא) which is "as was spoken." The Kaph (כ) is the prefix *as*. The word davara (דברא) is from the root word davar (דָּבַר), which means *speak* or *spoken* (Strong's H1696). Yes, this is the phrase commonly mispronounced *abracadabra*. Before you stop reading, hear me out.

---

3   Tenen, Stan. "Hebrew Alphabet Hand Gestures." © 1996. Meru Foundation. http://www.meru.org/Gestures/Atbashgest.html

This phrase should be pronounced *abracadavra,* and it contains the meaning, "I will create as it was spoken." In other words, I align my will to Yahweh's will to create what He has spoken into my scroll. Yahweh has written a scroll for each one of us. When we accept His will for our lives and decide to create what He has spoken concerning us, His glory shines through.

Elizabeth R. Corley

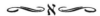

Eber expresses to me today that *Aleph* speaks from Yahweh's face as the Ox. Let us walk about Zion through our burden-bearer lowing our frequency of heaven.

Aaron Smith

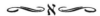

Aleph, the Strong Leader, bears our burdens and moves obstacles out of our path. He does this to lead us to glory. Aleph is made of two Yods and a Vav to begin the two worlds of above and below, with the peg, Vav, as the joint. Aleph creates with intent and reveals to us the creation process of breathing with intent. He leads us in our legislation from our seats in Zion. From the seat of responsibility with the ox-face, we bring the heavy glory of Yahweh to bear in the earth.

Teresa Bowen

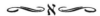

Aleph is the power of silence. It is where true strength originates. It carries the burden of trust. It doesn't shake its fist in the air and demand to be heard. It just is. Without saying a word, Aleph reveals the deepest of emotions and unmatched authority.

Y.A. Butler

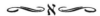

Aleph is the fullness of Yahweh. It is His leading, His strength, His breath, His promise, His fulfilment, His plan, and especially His love. In Aleph my journey begins, and in Aleph I find the completion of His word in my life. In Aleph I am royalty, I am seated, and adorned with the crown of Aleph.

Daniel Cook

BEYT

ב

MODERN

EARLY	MIDDLE	LATE

2

*B*eyt is Yahshua, the firm foundation. It is Him in me and me in Him. It is the ascended dwelling place.

Yahshua/firm foundation: Beyt is written with three Vavs—one to represent the roof, one to represent the side, and one the floor of a house or dwelling place. To ensure Beyt is not written like any other letter, the floor is extended beyond the side, emphasizing the foundation. I find it interesting that the late ancient Semitic/Hebrew form of Beyt (ℶ) also used three Vavs, but the roof was emphasized as having an upper balcony look. The present-day form of Beyt reflects that Yahshua the Messiah has come, and He is our firm foundation.

Him in me and me in Him: Beyt can act as a prefix meaning "in" before words. Beyt represents John 15:5 and John 17:22-23—Yahshua in me and me in Him.

Ascended dwelling place: Beyt was a house or tent floor plan in early ancient Semitic/Hebrew (◻). The word bah'·yith (בַּיִת) means house, dwelling habitation, shelter or abode (Strong's H1004). As Yahshua dwells in us, we become an ascended dwelling place—a dwelling place for the divine.

Elizabeth R. Corley

Eber reveals to me that *Beyt* is my speaking place, my place of safety and comfort, my place of unity and communion, my home. I thank you, Beyt, for representing and being this place that I can now speak from—and into—Mount Zion.

Aaron Smith

Beyt for me is the dwelling place, a safe and secure place. It speaks of family and of belonging. It is a spiritual house in which to dwell. It is the "many mansions" of our Father, Yahweh, where Yahshua has prepared a place for us. Beyt is all of us, humanity, in whom the Father dwells. It is the place of security in mystery.

Teresa Bowen

Beit is divinity/eternity/the *Olam* (עולם) which allows itself to be constricted (appearing to be restricted) and to be housed in human flesh, thus making what is hidden/unseen greater on the inside than it is on the outside.

Y.A. Butler

Beit is the first place of distinction. It is the place of Day (*yom* יום) and Night (*layil* ליל and *lewel* לול); the place of treasures lost, stolen and forfeited; the place of treasures found and restored. It is the House of Yahweh, a place of peace and rest. Beit is not a dichotomy: it is better understood by perspective. It can be seen as two sides of the same coin: the great and terrible Day of the Lord, and the darkness as unrevealed light where treasure is found and made tangible.

Daniel Cook

GIMAL

MODERN

EARLY	MIDDLE	LATE

3

Gimal is the camel, who carries the supply of heaven. He is running, walking, kneeling, and dealing bountifully to supply our needs, to truly help.

> Camel: Gimal was a camel or foot walking in the Early ancient Semitic/Hebrew (ʌ). The word gä·mäl' (גָּמָל) means *camel* (Strong's H1581).

> Supply of heaven: A camel carries supplies. Gimal represents a camel carrying the supplies Yahweh has for us.

> Running, walking, kneeling, and bountifully supplying: The running camel can be seen in Gimal's written form, with a Vav and a Yud. In late ancient Semitic/Hebrew, Gimal looks to me as if it is running (ʌ), with the Yud extended and pointing left. In modern Hebrew it looks as if it is walking (ג): the Yud is still extended pointing left, but is closer to the Vav. In some calligraphy of Gimal, the Yud is written as a flat short dot/line (ג).

I spent the summer of 2017 trying to learn calligraphy of the Hebrew letters. I did not like how Gimal was written. Late that summer, I took a trip to Florida for a family issue. I had the opportunity to see my adopted Jewish grandmother. She let me go through her Hebrew children's book collection and choose some for my class. One of the books I chose was about learning to read Hebrew. Flipping through the book, I came across Gimal. The previous student of the book had written a note: "kneeling camel." At that point, Yahweh revealed to me that Gimal is kneeling, ready for us to offload the supply of heaven. Before, Gimal was running and walking toward us. Now, Gimal is kneeling, ready for us to unpack the supplies we need, to truly help.

Elizabeth R. Corley

Eber is excited to reveal the joy of another letter, *Gimal*. Gimal is the transporter of earth's treasures to Heaven and Heaven's treasures to earth. Let us be joined to this amazing letter of Yahweh's expression of completeness.

Aaron Smith

Gimal is the third letter. The number three always speaks of completion and government, as seen in the Father, Son, and Holy Ghost, the bench of three. Gimal, the camel, represents the walking supply of heaven. Camels always remind me of the search for Isaac's bride. With ten camels, the servant of Abraham approaches a well and finds a beautiful young woman there fetching water. To his surprise, she gives him and his ten camels water. He knows she is the one to be Isaac's bride. The treasure the camels bore to give to the bride-to-be and her family are unloaded into her father's house. Rebecca, the young woman, is then loaded up on a camel to be taken back to marry Isaac. She was chosen to be the bride not only because of her outward beauty, but because of her heart, her care, and her nurturing. Daily, Yahweh sends out his dromedaries loaded with treasure. They come to those of us willing to give unto Him. Through Gimal, He brings His burden bearers rest and restoration from their journey. In other words, our acknowledgment of, engagement with, and heart of gratitude for Yahweh's walking supply and their assignment will bring the manifest provision in our lives.

Teresa Bowen

Gimmel is the unending supply from the wild and limitless resources via the Divine Chord that runs into and through us. It delivers its instantaneous payload for whatever and wherever the daily need may arise.

Y.A. Butler

Gimel is the journey of *olam*. It is the journey of dimensions and the journey of never-ending supply. Everything Yahweh is in you and everything you are in Him is supplied in Gimel.

Daniel Cook

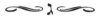

Dalet

ד

MODERN

EARLY	MIDDLE	LATE

4

*D*alet is a door, a pathway, a gate, a portal to realms, dimensions, dreams, and visions; it is always listening for the supply of heaven.

> Door, pathway, gate, portal to realms, dimensions, dreams and visions: Dalet was a tent door in early ancient Semitic/Hebrew (ﬢ). The Hebrew word *deh'·leth* (דֶּלֶת) means *door* or *gate* (Strong's H1817). I know Yahweh has a plan for my life, one of a hope and a future. When I seek His face, He opens doors, pathways and opportunities for me. He shows up glorious in my life. The dreams and visions He has given me become my reality.

> Always listening for the supply of heaven: Dalet is written with two Vavs. One represents the upper door post, and one represents the side door post. The corner where the two Vavs are joined is called an ear. Dalet reminds us as we stand at our tent door to listen and look for the supply of heaven which is brought by Gimal.

> *Elizabeth R. Corley*

As of late Eber has had me noticing the colors of the Seven Spirits shining in and through doors and door facings. Eber says that when you see the colors of the Seven Spirits, know that *Dalet* points to the reality that you are facing a chance to open or close something. Be aware of and honor Dalet as he introduces you to the portals of Yahweh.

Aaron Smith

Four is the number of the door. *Dalet* the door, or portal, is our access into the heavens. Yahshua is the door for us as sons of Yahweh. John chapter 10 states that anyone who comes through any door other than Yahshua is a thief. So, thus far we have engaged Aleph, the strong leader of the Beyt, or house, that is a walking supply of heaven, Gimal, that leads to the door, Dalet. Doors open into or out of, or they are closed and secured for safety.

Teresa Bowen

Dalet's humility speaks that it is not a door of arrival, but it is a door of doors… a gate of gates… an entrance and an exit… a coming to and a coming through. It's another marker in the eternal journey into Yahweh's evermore.

Y.A. Butler

Dalet is the place of choice. Yahshua is the door through which all is reconciled to the Father. First John 4:17 reveals that as He is in the earth, so are we (paraphrased). We are the portal between Heaven and earth, between the night *choshek* (חשך) and the day *yom* (יום). Bringing the mysteries of Yahweh into tangible evidence on the earth requires a door—a portal. It is with our hands outstretched that we bring about the *shefa* (שפע), the flow of the rivers of living water and unending supply into the earth.

Daniel Cook

HEY

ה

MODERN

EARLY	MIDDLE	LATE

5

Hey announces, "Look, behold: THE breath of Yahweh in me!" It is breathing in and out; it is being fully alive in Him. It is saying, *Heenayni* (הִנֵּנִי): "Here I am—fully present in body and mind, fully engaged."

Look, behold: The Hebrew word *hā* (הָא) means *behold* or *lo* (Strong's H1887). To behold something is to look at it. The early ancient Semitic/Hebrew of Hey (ψ) is a man with arms raised. It almost looks as if it is someone trying to get your attention. I think it's awesome that children naturally say, "Hey!" to get our attention, to get us to look at what they are doing. I know Yahweh wants me to look at and behold what He is doing and at what He wants me to do.

THE: Hey can be used as a prefix meaning *the*. For example, the Hebrew *Hashem* (הַשֵּׁם) means "The Name." *Hashem* is used to refer to Yahweh's Name, which is *Yod **Hey** Vav **Hey*** (יְהוָה). *Shem* (שֵׁם) is the Hebrew word for name.

Breath of Yahweh in me; breathing in and out: Hey has an /h/ sound as breathing out. The written letter Hey, ה, is formed from two Vavs (similar to Dalet) and an unattached Yud. It is important to have the opening, otherwise the letter would look like Chet: ח. The opening represents breathing in and out. "And the Lord God formed man of the dust of the ground, and breathed into his nostrils the breath of life; and man became a living soul" (Gen. 2:7). I desire to breathe in everything Yahweh has for me, all His words, and to breathe His words out to those in need. The late ancient Semitic/Hebrew Hey (ת) is closed, but its top line looks like flowing wind.

I believe Hey was expressing the four winds from Ezekiel 37:9.

> Then said he unto me, Prophesy unto the wind, prophesy, son of man, and say to the wind, Thus saith the Lord GOD; Come from the four winds, O breath, and breathe upon these slain, that they may live.

So, Hey is the Breath of Yahweh breathing. Today, Hey has the opening (ה), which I believe means that since Yahshua rent the veil, we can breathe in Yahweh's words and breathe them out to those in need.

Being fully alive in Him; saying *Heenayni* (הנני) here I am: To breathe in Yahweh's breath, His words, we must be fully engaged in His presence to love Him with all our heart, mind, and body (Deut. 6:5, Matt. 22:37, Mark 12:30, Luke 10:27).

Elizabeth R. Corley

Eber loves to introduce each letter as unique and above the rest. He is like a proud parent of the living letters. *Hey* is amazing, for it is the breath of Yahweh's life in our being—and it's in the name of Yahweh twice: *Yod **Hey** Vav **Hey***. Hey is the Christ in you, the hope of glory. We engage with Hey as the perfect one to help in awakening our minds and bodies. Let us breathe together His breath. HEY!

Aaron Smith

Hey is the breath of Divine Light that flows from us as we inhale and exhale from abiding in Yahweh and being seated in Zion. This letter is in the tetragrammaton, YHWH, or *Yod Hey Vav Hey*. Through Hey, the Creator's name arcs His breath to make manifest His delight.

Teresa Bowen

Hey speaks of divine respiration. Hey is the breath that empowers the voice and that gives life to the formed words. From Adam's first breath until Yahshua's last on the cross, Yahweh's Hey sings beginning and finishing. One breath folds into another—living soul into life-giving Spirit. The catalyst of Hey delivers within it wave after wave of life and energy, entering all dimensions at once. So, choose your words wisely.

Y.A. Butler

Hey ה: My word goes forth into all the earth and it will not return back to me void; it will accomplish all that I desire and it will prosper (Isa. 55:11, paraphrased). As Aleph can be seen as the breath of Yahweh, Hey can be seen as our breath returned back to Him. Hey frames what Yahweh has spoken. The form of the letter is seen as a Dalet and a Yod. Hey as a suffix makes a word feminine. As such, the Yod, the all-spark of Creation, is protected and formed in the Dalet until it is ready for birth. Hey frames the tangible evidence.

Daniel Cook

VAV

ו

MODERN

EARLY	MIDDLE	LATE
Y	✗	ו

6

*V**av* is man as a tent peg securing the heaven *and* earth connection.

> Man: Vav is the sixth letter of the Hebrew Aleph-Beyt. The number six represents man.

> Tent peg securing: The early ancient Semitic/Hebrew of Vav (Υ) is a tent peg. The Hebrew word *vä* (וָ) means hook, peg, nail, pin (Strong's H2053). A tent peg is used to secure a dwelling place.

> Heaven and earth connection – When writing the Hebrew letters, Vav is used in several other letters. It is considered to be an extended Yud, the dot now extended to be a line. So Vav is a vertical line, connecting heaven and earth.

> *And*: Vav can be used as a prefix meaning *and* before a word. Vav adds things together to create unity.

Elizabeth R. Corley

Eber reveals more of the significance of Yahweh's name and how it is made up of the letter *Vav*. Yahweh's name, again, is *Yod Hey **Vav** Hey*. Vav is the connector of the breath in us with His breath.

Aaron Smith

Vav is one of my favorite letters. It's an ascending and descending letter. Vav connects: it's the connector letter between heaven and earth. Vav joins together seemingly contradictory things, such as spirit and matter. This joining letter is in the tetragrammaton, *Yod Hey **Vav** Hey*.

Vav pegs truth and our scrolls to our soul, so that we are well-equipped to do the outworking we agreed to in Yahweh before we were sent to this earth.

Teresa Bowen

Vav speaks: "I am the stabilizing factor of the six dimensions. North, south, east, and west… the up and the down. I am the bridge between things that oppose themselves. I am man. I am planted. When the tabernacle of the Almighty is stretched out, I am the peg that holds it in its place."

Y.A. Butler

Vav is the security and establishment of Yahweh's word in the earth—it is the heaven and earth connection, and the very heart of His focus. Vav also represents man.

Daniel Cook

ZAYIN

MODERN

EARLY	MIDDLE	LATE

7

Zayin is a tool for nourishing or cutting, a plow or a sword. It is a scribe's pen, speaking of purpose as Kings and Priests: it is the crowned Vav.

> Tool for nourishing or cutting, a plow or a sword: The early ancient Semitic/Hebrew of Zayin (⹉) is similar to a mattock, which could be used as a weapon or as a tool to break up the ground, like a plow. So Zayin represents a tool used for a purpose. Yahweh has a plan, a purpose, a hope and future for each one of us (Jer. 29:11).

> Scribe's pen: In modern Hebrew, Zayin looks like a scribe's pen. This is particularly meaningful to me, as I know Yahweh has called me to teach. I have tried to adhere to Habakkuk 2:1-2,

>> I will stand upon my watch, and set me upon the tower, and will watch to see what he will say unto me, and what I shall answer when I am reproved. And the LORD answered me, and said, Write the vision, and make it plain upon tables, that he may run that readeth it.

> I look to see what Yahweh will say concerning the letters and write it plainly, so the reader can quickly understand the purpose of the letters.

> Speaking of purpose as Kings and Priests; the crowned Vav: In writing the calligraphy form of Zayin, a line (Vav) is written and then a small diagonal line is placed on its top (a crown). So, Zayin is considered a crowned Vav (ז) – Man with a crown. We are called a royal priesthood (1 Pet. 2:9) that we should show forth the praises of Yahweh.

Elizabeth R. Corley

35

In the light of being seated in Zion as of September 22, 2017, Eber says *Zayin's* position looks different and more distinct than it did before our seating. He's in a dimensional shift just as we have been. The following is some of his new role: he is a transporter of time for the sake of food for life of the spirit to affect the physical. He's the destroyer of the restrictions of time infractions.

Aaron Smith

Zayin, the seventh letter, is to me the first letter that gives way to descending. It is the first crowned letter. Hebrew sages say it's the Vav with a crown. There is a mystery in this letter Zayin. It represents the "Christed Man," the seated, crowned man. In essence, Zayin represents glorified sons who ascend and descend to rule and bring justice and order to the earth and the cosmos. It is said that Zayin represents time and/or a weapon and nourishment. So, given this definition, I see the Word of Yahweh sharper than a two-edged sword that nourishes us, spirit, soul and body. Zayin is the root to remember, so with the Seven Spirits we ask Zayin to help us remember our beginning, the *Adam Kadmon*, the crowned man before the fall. "Energy cannot be created or destroyed, it can only be changed from one form to another" (Einstein). As Yahweh's creation, we can only go from one form of energy to another as in a glory to glory form as Yahweh's Word has promised.

Teresa Bowen

Zayin is the time lord. He remembers. He walks the time-line plowing. He uncovers the hidden. With each step, he brings to remembrance generational blessings or ties of iniquity. You allow him to feed/nourish them or destroy/cut them off because of your divine right to choose.

Y.A. Butler

Zayin is the crown of authority. Zayin is a crowned Vav and looks like a scepter and a crown. Zayin, as the 7th letter in the Aleph-Beit, also represents time. The seventh day is *Shabbat* שבת or Sabbath, the day of rest and peace. I can't help but believe that this letter is very significant. We have been seated with a scepter and crown in the ages of peace.

Daniel Cook

CHET

ח

MODERN

EARLY	MIDDLE	LATE

8

Chet is a tent wall representing a separation from the outside, for the yoking between Yashua and us. It is Zayin and Vav connected. It is evermore life, *Chayei Olam* (חיי עולם).

Tent wall: The early ancient Semitic/Hebrew of Chet, (𐤇) is a tent wall. A tent wall divides the inside from the outside. The Hebrew word *khüts* (חוץ) (Strong's H2351) means outside, separated by a wall. Yahweh is holy and has called us to be holy, set apart as sacred.

The yoking: One Hebrew calligraphy styling of Chet (חַ) is written as a Zayin and Vav connected by a thin line. Consider the Zayin to represent Yahshua, and Vav to represent us. Chet reminds us that we are to be joined to Yahshua and that we are joint-heirs with Christ (Rom. 8:17).

Evermore life, חיי עולם, *Chayei Olam*: Chet begins the Hebrew *khah'·ē* (חַי) meaning *life*. Yahshua said that "He that believeth on me hath everlasting life" (John 6:47). The Hebrew for *everlasting life* is *Chayei Olam*. *Chayei* means "life of." *Olam* means everlasting, evermore, eternity; time out of mind; ancient, world, and universe. Olam is not just a time concept but also a space concept. In other words, in Olam, there is neither end nor beginning. When we are joined to Yahshua, believe in Him, and engage with Him, we have life of everlasting.

Elizabeth R. Corley

I sense Eber's joy in presenting the letter *Chet*. Chet is the combination of Zayin, the one that lassos time, and Vav, the one that connects us from Heaven to earth. He reveals to us that time desires to work for us who engage and believe in this great place of Zion and this will bring the glorious change that reflects Heaven on earth. *Chet* is the 8th letter that witnesses the four corners of Heaven and earth. Awesome!

Aaron Smith

Chet is the letter that speaks of a new beginning. It is the letter that speaks of life, *chai*. Eber tells me Chet is the life-bringer of new beginnings into my life, my yard, as it is the letter that speaks of a boundary, of what's inside and what's out. In Chet, you see the two previous letters connected: the Zayin, the Crowned Man with the sword of the Spirit, the yoke that connects, and the Vav, which is Man. Like a great archway, Chet the invitation to pursue a new and miraculous path beyond current borders.

Teresa Bowen

Chet is a hilarious letter! It is full of laughter. It is the joy spring of vibrant health and vitality. Chet keeps you, surrounds you. Chet's joy is the fabric of life.

Y.A. Butler

Chet means boundary, or skin. As of late, I have been seeing Chet as our secret place with Yahweh, a universe of two and a universe of many, all in the place of Now. Chet is the hovering letter—touching, yet not touching, under the Shadow of the Almighty. It is the place of *Yom* and *Choshek*. It is the place of the hidden treasure. It is the place of Up Here!

Daniel Cook

TET

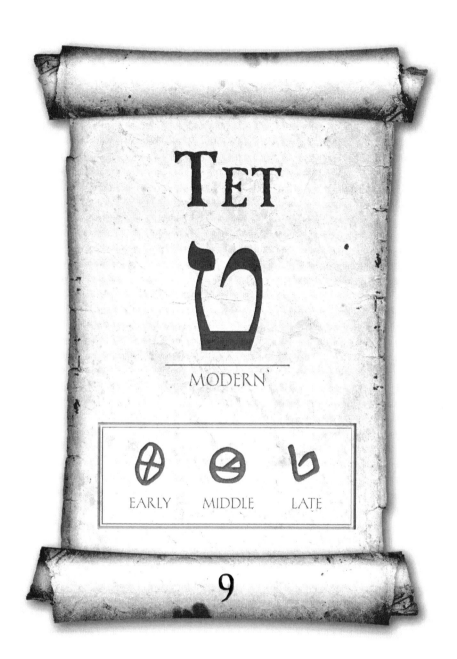

MODERN

EARLY	MIDDLE	LATE

9

Tet is our basket, blessed by Yahweh, if we will hearken diligently unto His voice (Deut. 28:1, 5), as being wrapped in and surrounded by His voice.

> Basket: The Early ancient Semitic/Hebrew of Tet (𝚹) is a basket. A basket contains items that are needed.

> Blessed by Yahweh, if we will hearken diligently unto His voice (Deut. 28:1, 5): In Deuteronomy 28:5, the Hebrew word for *basket* is teh'·neh (טֶנֶא) (Strong's H2935). When our baskets are blessed by Yahweh, those containers are surrounded (ט) by continual (נ) strength (א).

> Being wrapped in and surrounded by His voice: The Hebrew word *tallit* (טַלִּית) begins with the letter Tet. A tallit is a fringed cloth as known as a prayer shawl. The root word of tallit is tä·lal' (טָלַל), which means *cover* (Strong's H2926). Tallit symbolizes the covering of Yahweh and being surrounded by Him. We listen for His voice, His sound, as we are surrounded by Him.

> *Elizabeth R. Corley*

Eber reveals to me that *Tet* is exceptional in its place and position. Tet is usually interpreted as representing the good and evil of man, but in the Up Here of Zion, it has somewhat of a different role. Tet, in Zion, reveals the great/good and terrible/evil of what we will be as we release Yahweh's sounds and faces from our speaking places. These sounds and decrees declare the glory of Yahweh into all earth. Hallelujah!

Aaron Smith

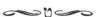

43

Tet is the basket and what is in that basket is determined by each of us individually. The basket contains what we engage in, natural and spiritual, whether good or evil. As Yahweh's sons, engaging in His Kingdom World of the Up Here, our basket is filled with His abundant life, His glory, and mystery. Engaging Tet, from our basket we will draw out the intent of our hearts.

Teresa Bowen

Tet is a letter of accountability. What's in your basket? Tet speaks of responsibility and stewardship. You take ownership in what you allow.

Y.A. Butler

Tet, ט, is the good contained within. Tet represents a basket and a place of choice. I choose what to put in the basket of "me." For this reason, the tallit (טלית) has become important to me. In this secret place of Yahweh, under the tallit, I fill my basket with Him. I choose to live and remain (*olam,* עולם) under His tallit (טלית).

Daniel Cook

YUD

י

MODERN

EARLY	MIDDLE	LATE

10

Yud is the dot, the atom, the spark of Ruach Yahweh in every letter and in everything.

The dot, or atom: Yud is the smallest letter of the Aleph-Beyt. It's like the atom of all the letters.

Spark of Ruach Yahweh: The early ancient Semitic/Hebrew of Yud (ﯨﯩ) is an arm and hand. The Hebrew word *yäd* (יָד) means *hand* and *power* (Strong's H3027). Yud represents Yahweh delivering us with a strong hand and an outstretched arm (Psalm 136:12); it is Yahweh traversing the universe in a micro-instant. Yud can be used as a prefix meaning "he will." This reminds us of Yahweh's will for our lives and His promises.

In every letter and everything: Hebrew scribes consider that once a pen is set to paper, a Yud is written. Therefore, every letter starts with a Yud. We can conclude that every written word also starts with the pen to paper, therefore all writing starts with some form of Yud. The Hebrew word *dä·vär'* (דָּבָר) means *word* and also *thing* (Strong's H1697). Every word and thing contains some form of Yud.

Elizabeth R. Corley

Yod is the first letter that Yahweh revealed to me. At first, I had no idea what Yod was other than a dot. Then, Yahweh asked me to "connect the dots" of what He had taught me. I first thought it was an expression, but later I knew He meant it literally. The dots were actually Yods and were the eyes around the wheels within the wheels of Ezekiel's vision (Ezek. 1:16-18).

Yod is now in everything I see and do with the letters, for they begin and finish the paths that lead to the treasures of Yahweh's Word. I love Yod, and I am grateful for the paths we are now on together. Thank you, Yod, for being my friend.

Aaron Smith

Yod, the dot, the letter that sits in all the letters, as the dot must be made to bring about all the other written letters. It's the tenth letter, yet the first in the execution of writing all the letters. This seemingly small dot is so significant that nothing begins without its power to race across the multiverses in a micro-instant to perform and finish a task. It is the action of thought-speed to bring the painting of the big picture in one's mind. This letter Yod begins the tetragrammaton, **Yod Hey Vav Hey**. The spelling of Yod is *Yod Vav Dalet*, which reveals the significance of it traversing through width, depth, and up and down.

Teresa Bowen

Yod is the spark of change. By the time you've blinked, Yod has gone to the other side of the universe and back again. Just that quickly, its momentum instigates transformation. It's the power of worship. It brings walls down and opens prison doors. It is also the power of the little things added up. It is the faithful works of our hands allowing us to be finishers.

Y.A. Butler

Yod (׳) is creative light. It is the all-spark of creation. It is the dot. All that is written begins with a dot; all of the letters begin with a Yod. John 1:1-5 says:

In the beginning was the Word, and the Word was with God, and the Word was God. The same was in the beginning with God. All things were made by him; and without him was not any thing made that was made. In him was life; and the life was the light of men. And the light shineth in darkness; and the darkness comprehended it not.

Yashua is our *Yod*. This same Yod is the seed of our dreams, the all-spark of His word manifested in our lives. It is the responsibility of care and the path to maturity. In this unique place that we have as sons of Almighty Yahweh on this earth, Yod sets us as royalty and sees the completed work, when we are still in process. This place is called Now. His name is Yod.

Daniel Cook

KAPH

כ

MODERN

EARLY   MIDDLE   LATE

11

Khaf is a picture of the palm of the hand. It is blessing and calling forth the potential within for manifestation in the actual. On Yahweh's palm, He has engraved and inscribed us.

> Palm of the hand: The Early ancient Semitic/Hebrew of *Khaf* (𑁋) is palm of the hand. The Hebrew word *kaf* (כַּף) means *hollow hand* or *palm* (Strong's H3709).

> Blessing and calling forth the potential within for the manifestation: When a father blesses a child, he places the palm of his hand on the child's head. The blessing or declaration calls forth the potential within the child to be manifested in the actual.

> On Yahweh's palm, He has engraved, inscribed us: "Behold, I have graven thee upon the palms of my hands; thy walls are continually before me" (Is. 49:16). We are inscribed, written on Yahweh's palms.

> *Elizabeth R. Corley*

Kaph contains much depth. It represents the open palm of your hand. Eber reminded me of the reference to "clean hands" in Psalm 24. The Psalmist asks, "Who may ascend unto the hill of the Lord? Or who may stand in his holy place?" (v.3). The next verse answers the questions: "He who has clean hands [*Kaph*] and a pure heart; who has not lifted up his soul to vanity, nor sworn deceitfully" (v.4). Eber is revealing the depths of the open palm that lead to the depths of the soul. When we lay hands on someone in prayer, we are giving out of the depths of our souls. First Timothy 5:22 warns against laying hands on someone suddenly. The hand, in this case, is imparting and identifying purity.

I do not believe Kaph is present if purity isn't present. I believe we have missed the mark of understanding of Kaph until now, but in this mountain we must call upon The Spirit of Understanding in order to reach the depths of Yahweh's greatness. Kaph, thank you for connecting the depths of our understanding to our purpose.

Aaron Smith

The *Kaf*, or palm of the hand, speaks to me of sending forth with blessings. I stand with hands raised to the heavens, with open palms, to activate my earth, the heavens, and the heaven of heavens! Kaf reminds me of Apostle F. Nolan Ball saying, "I will hold in my heart the Word of promise, until I hold it in my hand." Kaf speaks of the tangible evidence of spiritual activations and engagements in our lives. Kaf speaks of our Father Yahweh's hand upon our head as a crown of blessing. The letter Kaf begins the word *kavōd*. The words glory, honor, and respect define *kavōd*.

Teresa Bowen

Kaf is the response of heaven through us. We are the gloves, Yahweh the hand. Kaf is unity in action, and my intention and willpower married to His purpose. We then become a physical demonstration and manifestation of "no greater love" (John 15:13).

Y.A. Butler

Kaf means the palm of the hands. As I take my own hands and cup them side by side, in a gesture of giving, behold, I am presenting a completed work. We are the works of the hands of Yahweh, yet we are responsible to allow Him to complete His work in us, as we present our lives back to Him. Behold: Your sons.

Daniel Cook

ך

KHAF FINAL

Khaf Final represents standing and taking your position to finish the purpose Yahweh has placed in you.

Standing: Khaf Final (ך) is the first of five final *sofit* (סופית) or ending letters. The finals only occur at the end of a word. Khaf (כ) is written differently at the end of a word. Instead of appearing as a half circle or bent line, it is written with two Vavs, similar to Dalet (ד), but the side Vav of Khaf final extends below the base line of the text. It looks as if Khaf is standing and reaching below. Khaf final's extended line reminds us that as we have been blessed by the hand of Yahweh, we need to bless others in need.

Your: Khaf final can be used as a suffix meaning *your*. It indicates we have a responsibility for and ownership in finishing what has been given to us. This can be seen in Deuteronomy 6:7, which states: "You shall teach them diligently *to your children* (לְבָנֶיךָ), and shall talk of them when you sit *in your house* (בְּבֵיתֶךָ), when you walk by the way, when you lie down, and when you rise up."

Elizabeth R. Corley

Kaph, the King:

This king mirrors Heaven. *Kaph Final* is a king of glory. By the purity of his hands and heart, he will occupy his inheritance. His territory is enlarged by understanding, wisdom, and diligence. This king extends his hand in justice to the poor and hears the cry of the widow and the orphan. He lifts the heads of the broken and banquets in the presence of his enemies.

Y.A. Butler

Kaph Final is like a mirror. On one side stands the shell of a reflection of what I want the world to see. On the other stands the fullness of His word, His scroll—the reflection of His purposes in me. As I stand before this mirror and look into the fullness of His Word and purpose in me, reading the scroll of all Yahweh has said of me, I am transfigured from the shell of my own making into a mature son possessing all He has made me to be. I have become what I behold, which is His reflection! I am standing as Kaph Final.

Daniel Cook

LAMED

MODERN

EARLY	MIDDLE	LATE

12

*L*amed is to learn and teach with a heart that understands true knowledge, to be spurred to action.

To learn and teach: Lamed can be used as a prefix meaning *to*. The Hebrew word *lä·mad'* (לָמַד) means *learn* and also *teach* (Strong's H3925). I find that I truly have not learned something until I can teach it to someone else. I can read or study something, but not until I can impart it, do I truly know it.

With a heart that understands true knowledge; spurred to action: The early ancient Semitic/Hebrew of Lamed (𐤋) is a shepherd's staff. A shepherd's staff is used to goad sheep toward something, so it represents a spurring to action. The Hebrew *läv* (לֵב) means *heart* (Strong's H3820). Ours hearts are meant to be the teacher (ל) of our house (ב). We need to be lead by Holy Ghost, the Spirit of Understanding, and the Spirit of Knowledge, so we can understand true knowledge. So, Lamed is the knowledge that spurs us to action.

Psalm 25:4 - Your ways, Yahweh, show me Your paths teach me (lä·mĕ·dā·nē לְמַדֵנִי).

This is my heart's cry. Lamed is in both my names: the name my parents gave me, Elizabeth, el·ē·sheh'·vah (אֱלִישֶׁבַע), meaning "my God has sworn" (Strong's H472), and the name Yahweh has revealed to me (להבצוד), "a heart that understands the breath of the dwelling place of the Divine, (staying on) the righteous path securing portals," which is pronounced lah'·hav tsüd, flame hunt (Strong's H3851 & H6679). Lamed reminds me to hunt out the flames that Yahweh wants me to learn and teach.

Elizabeth R. Corley

Eber introduces *Lamed* to me with him in his hand. I see Eber walking with Lamed as with a shepherd's staff, but also pointing with him, as if Lamed is showing him the way. What I'm seeing looks similar to the fable of the water diviner's rod that could identify where water could be found for a water well. I see Eber and Lamed working together to accomplish a goal, or find a path to a treasure. Lamed represents the teacher side of the Spirit of Knowledge. Lamed works well with the Spirit of Knowledge and the Spirit of Understanding. Let us engage with Lamed, as Eber does. He is alive. Thank you, Eber.

Aaron Smith

Lamed is revealing to me his desire to teach and to be taught. His double function is key for us. We learn to teach, to keep the revelation flowing to the generations to come. Lamed is taller than the rest of the living letters because he rallies all to the truth of all that the Father intends for us to walk in.

Teresa Bowen

Lamed is a heart that has stood the test of time. He has weathered many a storm. He is not afraid because he is anchored on solid rock. He extends up into the heavens becoming a beacon and guide to others. His strength is in his purity. He is willing to quietly learn—no matter how much he already knows.

Y.A. Butler

Lamed is the voice of the teacher, the voice of the strong leader. Lamed is one who rises above and sees from a new perspective, one who cries out from the Heart of Yahweh, and one who looks like his Father. Lamed is a letter of transcendence. A teacher must transcend himself and see through the eyes of his student to convey ascended thought in the manner the student sees and understand. So Lamed transcends heaven and earth to rise above and see beyond.

Daniel Cook

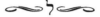

MEM

MODERN

| EARLY | MIDDLE | LATE |

*M**em** is water. It is a vibrating, vast sea of mysteries waiting for us to search out things hidden and secrets to be revealed.

> Water, vibrating: The early ancient Semitic/Hebrew of Mem (ᗰ) is water. To me, it looks like a frequency reading on a meter that reflects vibration.

> A vast sea of mysteries waiting...: The Hebrew word *mah'*·yim (מַיִם) means *water* (Strong's H4325). The Hebrew word *me* (מִי) is a question word meaning *who*, *whose*, or *whom* (Strong's H4310). Mem can be used as a suffix to make a word plural. So *mah'*·yim (מַיִם) could be broken down as a plural of *me* (מִי), meaning "many questions." Mem is like a vast sea of many questions: mysteries, secrets and hidden things. Daniel 2:22 says of Yahweh, "He revealeth the deep and secret things: he knoweth what is in the darkness, and the light dwelleth with him." Proverbs 25:2 says, "It is the glory of God to conceal a thing: but the honour of kings is to search out a matter."

Mem reminds us to search out the hidden things, the riddles, and mysteries Yahweh has for us.

Elizabeth R. Corley

Eber reveals to us that the letter *Mem* represents the depths and potential troubling of the waters. Mem is made up of Kaph and Vav, and therefore speaks of the depths of the heart pegged into the depths of the earth. Mem represents water. If you look at the top of the letter, it appears to be a wave. The Spirit of Wisdom goes hand in hand with Mem for she is from the depths of the Father Yahweh.

Aaron Smith

Mem speaks of the never-ending supply of heaven, our inheritance, and part of our makeup. *Adam,* a word we recognize from Hebrew, is made up of the letters *Aleph Dalet Mem.* Together, they show us that *Adam,* man, is the strong leader of the door to the never-ending supply of heaven. With this revelation "Vaved" to our cellular memory, we will make the worlds a glorious place.

Teresa Bowen

Mem is the essence of the upper and lower waters… the depths… a mixing of blood and water. Mem is mystery. There may be chaos on the surface of a stormy sea and even loud raging where the shallows meet the shore, but deep, deep down in the depths is the mystery of the hidden life.

Y.A. Butler

Mem is the voice of many waters. Just as this letter means water, and water is made of many drops, so it is with Mem. Each drop has a place, and each drop contains supply. As we come together in Mem, flowing in Yahweh, we bring with us the supply of heaven.

Daniel Cook

MEM FINAL

*M***em Final** is a finished, complete connection. It is numerous waters.

Complete connection: The calligraphy Mem (מ) is written as a Vav (ו) leaning on a Khaf (כ). An opening at the bottom reflects this leaning. The calligraphy Mem final (ם) is written with the Khaf and Vav completed and connected: there is no opening. Mem Final reminds us of unity. It is man completely engaged with the palm of Yahweh.

Note: Mem Final should not be confused with Samech, which forms a complete circle (ס). Mem Final (ם) has a square shape.

Numerous waters: Mem Final can be used as a suffix to make the word plural, numerous. In that way, Mem Final reminds us of many waters. It represents the many mysteries Yahweh has for us to search out.

Elizabeth R. Corley

Mem, the Oracle:

Mem Final, the Oracle, is a keeper of mysteries. It is an enclosed womb of the Word. It is the secret treasure-bearer. It is suspended in the deep waters, waiting to be drawn out. This is the only letter that does not stand tall because it protects its contents.

It is closed off to those who do not Honor.

Y.A. Butler

Pondering an image of a vast great ocean, I begin to consider the complexities that make up that ocean. Each drop is intricately connected to the other, despite the great expanse. Each drop contains a treasure. In that treasure is a deep cry to join the treasure of the one drop to the expanse of the great ocean, creating in Yahweh the supply of the fullness of Heaven. *Mem Final* is the supply of Heaven out to the greatest expanse being found in all of us.

Daniel Cook

NUN

נ

MODERN

EARLY   MIDDLE   LATE

14

Nun means to continue. It means to propagate life: it is a sprouted seed. It is the faithful and righteous man.

Continue, propagate life: The Hebrew word *nün* (נוּן) means continue, to increase, propagate (Strong's H5125).

Sprouted seed: The early ancient Semitic/Hebrew of Nun (➤) is a sprouted seed.

Faithful and righteous man: Nun is written as a Vav bent with a crown like Zayin. Nun represents a faithful son of Yahweh kneeling. The word *nün* (נוּן) is spelled *Nun Vav Nun*. When Nun is written at the end of a word, it is written with the Vav extending below the base line. It is as if the Nun is standing upright, representing an upright, righteous son of Yahweh.

Elizabeth R. Corley

Eber presents *Nun* as the righteous one that humbly but confidently stands upright for the sake of perpetuity. *Nun* is not only gracious but graceful in its position of royalty due to its inheritance by the blood of the Lamb of God that has taken away all disloyal and disgraceful alliances. *Nun* stands tall, proclaiming our position and place in Heaven and Earth for all eternity. Amazing!

Aaron Smith

Nun is the multiplicity of the heirs of Yahweh and the joint-heirs with Christ. "Multiplying what?" you might ask. The biggest part of Nun that speaks to me is that this letter begins the words *navooah* (prophecy), *navi* (prophet), and *niggun* (melody/tune).

So, what we as heirs speak, breathe, sing, and meditate on, is what we will multiply, because it is an inherited power within us that just is.

Teresa Bowen

Nun is the fullness of a SON. It carries within the power of inheritance. He is the spiritual, nuclear potential that transitions faith to fulfillment. He enjoys the challenge of searching out the mysteries of the depths because he is made for it. He is not assuming and lazy, but an active participant in divine exploration.

Y.A. Butler

Nun is the faithful, humble prince. Nun is comprised of a Vav with a crown placed on his head, yet he is bent over in humility. Nun is a picture of Yahshua's teaching that the greatest among you will be the servant of all (Mark 10:44). This humility is not the false humility of abasement, but the heart of love in service to all. O, crowned prince, you are faithful!

Daniel Cook

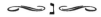

NUN FINAL

*N***un Final** represents the upright, righteous son standing, finishing their purpose.

> Upright, righteous son standing: Nun Final (ן) is written as a Vav extended below the baseline of the text. It reminds us of a son standing, ready to do the will of the Father.

> Their: Nun Final can be used as a suffix meaning *their*. As Nun Final is written at the end of a word, finishing the word, it reminds us that righteous sons finish their purpose given by Yahweh.

Elizabeth R. Corley

Nun, the Son:

Nun Final is co-heir with Christ. He enjoys the position of inheritance because he understands the process of obedience to and correction by Yahweh. This is a son of Honor. This son carries the tenacious seed that doesn't stop growing no matter how much it's cut down. This is the mature son who multiplies blessings and gifts for the next generation.

Y.A. Butler

To get to know *Nun Final*, consider Galatians 4:1-7.

> Now I say, That the heir, as long as he is a child, differeth nothing from a servant, though he be lord of all; But is under tutors and governors until the time appointed of the father. Even so we, when we were children, were in bondage under the elements of the world: But when the fulness of the time was come, God sent forth his Son, made of a woman, made under the law, To redeem them that were under the law, that we might receive the adoption of sons. And because ye are sons, God hath sent forth the Spirit of his Son into your hearts, crying, Abba, Father. Wherefore thou art no more a servant, but a son; and if a son, then an heir of God through Christ.

A young prince, already made the ruler of all, discovers his identity is not manifest in his position, but in his relationship. In the fullness of time—he is a son—and that time is NOW!

Daniel Cook

SAMECH

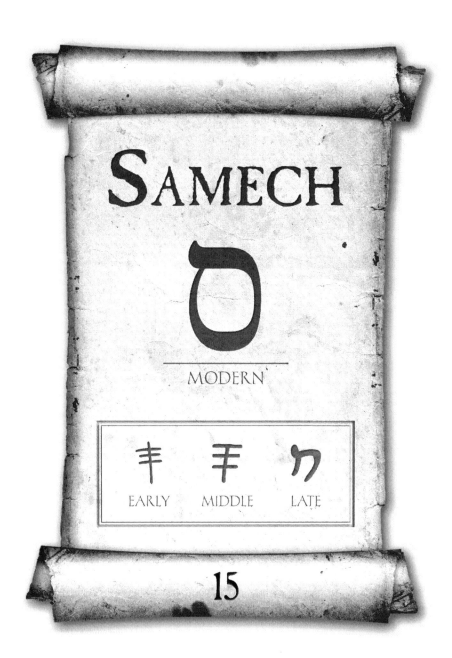

MODERN

EARLY	MIDDLE	LATE

Samech is support. It is Yahweh's protection encircling Mount Zion.

> Support: The early ancient Semitic/Hebrew of Samech (﬩) is a shield as a thorn bush. The Hebrew word *sä·mak'* (סָמַךְ) *means to lean, lay, rest, support, put, uphold, lean upon* (Strong's H5564). Samech represents Yahweh's support.

> Yahweh's protection, circled in mount Zion (צִיּוֹן): The modern Samech is written as a circular shape with a square left corner. Samech represents Yahweh's protection encircling His sons in Mount Zion.

> *Elizabeth R. Corley*

Eber desires for *Samech* to reveal its hidden position and place. While Samech represents a shield and protector of Yahweh through the power of Yahshua and His name, Samech desires also to show its purpose for this great age. It's shaped like a shield, but if we can see it in other dimensions, we see a spiraling path of light. The path of light leads our way into *choshek*, the place of the deep darkness of Yahweh. Samech in this age represents the path to the treasures of the day that will forever deliver and protect us from the slaveries of man's flesh. Hallelujah!

Aaron Smith

Samek begins the word *sookim* (ladder; inner-journeying). The mystery of Samek is that it speaks of divine support and a spiraling staircase or ladder. I find I get my support from ascending into the heavens, into my Father's house of many mansions, and into the river of life before the throne on the sea of glass.

And there is where I find everything that I need for everything that is required of me. Samek is the only letter that makes a complete circle.

Teresa Bowen

Samech is a picture of divine support to work and be the impossible. Samech demonstrates the healthy, daily dependence on Yahweh's grace and mercy. Yahweh is the staff I lean on, the hand I hold on to. Samech reminds me that I must be *in* Christ in order to remain *Up* Here. Without Him, I can do nothing.

Y.A. Butler

Samech is supernatural support. It is the wheel within a wheel. Samech is the only Hebrew letter that is completely enclosed. An ancient Hebrew midrash says when Yahweh wrote on the first sapphire tablets Moses brought down from a secret place on top of Mount Sinai, the letters went completely through the entire stone tablet. As Samech is a circle, Yahweh supernaturally supported the center of Samech and did not allow its center to fall out. We are that center and are meant to fill the space between the inner and outer circle. As we draw near to Him, He draws near to us. The center is now full, and none can tell there was ever a gap. Now, let us be formed to the express image of Yahweh and fill that circle. Let us be Him in the earth.

Daniel Cook

AYIN

MODERN

| EARLY | MIDDLE | LATE |

16

*A*yin is the eye, a fountain, a well. It means to see, to understand, and obey. Ayin shows us to meditate on the fountain of profound mysteries.

> Eye, fountain, well: The early ancient Semitic/Hebrew of Ayin (⬤) is an eye. The Hebrew word *ah'·yin* (עַיִן) means *an eye* or *fountain* (Strong's H5869 & h5870).

> To see, understand, and obey: "The best teachers are those who show you where to look, but don't tell you what to see." [4] To me, looking and seeing are two different things. You can look at something, but not understand it. To see something is not just to look at it. True seeing is understanding and then applying that understanding.

> To meditate on the fountain of profound mysteries: The Hebrew word *shä·mah'* (שָׁמַע) means "to hear intelligently, listen to, obey" (Strong's H8085). In order to truly hear something, we need to consume (שׁ) the frequency (מ) we see (ע). Yes: the frequency we *see.*

Hearing is not just with our ears, but also with our eyes. We need to understand and meditate on what is being heard and seen, and then put it into action. Yahweh has mysteries for us to search out (Prov. 25:2).

Elizabeth R. Corley

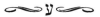

Ayin is one of the first letters that became my friend. He introduced himself some time ago, revealing paths into the dimensions. Eber expounds on how Ayin helped save the ancient portal path of Ghah.

---

4   The quotation is from a popular internet meme frequently attributed to "Alexandra K. Trenfor."

He did this by blending Ghah within himself in order to hide secret paths that are in him. Ayin had the dimensional ability to confuse the Babylonians from finding the depths of the night paths that lead to *choshek*. Ayin is the giver of himself for the cause of the Kingdom. He has great respect from all the other letters. Every decree I write and every new law devised for the Up Here place must always go through Ayin for he is the portal to the dimensions. I am thankful for you and honor you, Ayin.

Aaron Smith

Ayin is one of my favorite living letters. Ayin carries so much mystery and so much provision. Throughout this process of learning and meditating on the meanings and digging into the depths of the letters, I see throughout them the same thread of life, connected and flowing. Ayin in its purest form is the eye and its meaning is the fountain, two seemingly disconnected functions. Ayin speaks of the interconnectedness of all things and the hidden mysteries therein. The fountain speaks of the center of the landscape, of what is flowing forth from my life, what I see and what pours forth from my life. We find in Strong's H5869 the words *fountain* and *eyes* to be *ayin* and they have the same Hebrew meaning. The word *ayin* itself speaks volumes. *Ayin Yud Nun*: my eye, my spiritual and mental faculties, spring forth and traverse the universe in a micro-instant, to materialize and multiply what I focus on and engage with as an heir of Yahweh.

Teresa Bowen

Ayin is insight, discernment and perception. Ayin sees around corners and all sides at once. She is powerful because she changes your judgment and gives you the ability to see the bigger picture. She is a letter of empathy, allowing you to see through the eyes of another. Her discernment gives you the ability to "see" what the Father is saying. Her warning side is that you become what you behold.

Y.A. Butler

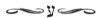

Ayin and *Pey* (the next letter) go together as a single poem.

Ayin

I see as you reveal to me all that I have always been.

As Your word removes the veils of my own making, my heart reflects our depths.

The revelation, the perfection of Your love that has brought me to this place.

Pey

Your word explodes like a river from the depths of who I am.

My mouth declares what my eyes behold.

The Glory of the secret place.

The place of just You and me.

Daniel Cook

PEY

MODERN

EARLY	MIDDLE	LATE

17

*P*ey is the mouth and insight's expression.

> Mouth: The early ancient Semitic/Hebrew of Pey (ᔃ) is a mouth. The Hebrew word *peh* (פֶּה) is *mouth* (Strong's H6310).

> Insight's expression: First, see (Ayin) to understand and obey, then speak (Pey) to release a spiritual energy into the universe.

Ayin comes before Pey in the AlephBeyt to remind us that we need to see first and then speak. In speaking, we release a frequency that effects both the seen and unseen.

Elizabeth R. Corley

✦✦✦

Now that we have been seated in Zion, most everything has changed in perspective of purpose. I find the Hebrew letters have taken on the purpose of revealing the hidden mysteries that Yahweh desires to unveil. They are showing another side of themselves from within the mountain. *Pey* is no exception. Pey is presented by Eber as the mouth or place of speaking. Our throne rooms in Zion are just that—speaking places. Pey is at home here in this place more than ever—that is, since the creation. As we decree and speak from our throne rooms, let us honor this great letter. As we do, our words will be released from the depths to the greater depths. Amazing!

Aaron Smith

✦✦✦

Pey may appear to be insignificant: however, scripture reveals the importance of our words and how we say them. Pey is the mouth, the opening, the portal of release for our breath and words into the atmosphere and the hearer. Pey means to blow/ to scatter.

The blowing from this portal releases spiritual energy into the universe, setting into motion things seen and unseen. I, for one, have had to think about my words and my tone. I still do. It is a process that I take very seriously. I want what is manifesting in my life and my loved ones' lives and eternity to be a blessing.

Teresa Bowen

Pey is the mouth; the seat of choice. What do I choose to plant with my mouth: life or death? As I take in breath and release sound, I send seeds/sparks through this gate of transformation. I create fruit I will eat and feed to others.

Y.A. Butler

(For *Pey*, see entry under *Ayin*.)

Daniel Cook

PEY FINAL

*P*ey *Final* represents spoken words standing upright and open.

> Standing upright and open: Pey (פ) is written as a Khaf with an ascending Yud. Pey Final (ף) is written similarly, but instead of a curved Khaf, Pey Final is only curved at the top, and the line extends below the baseline of the text. It reminds us of an upright open mouth, bringing truth and praise.
>
> *Elizabeth R. Corley*

Pey, the Legislator:

> The Books are open. Now what you say is law. It is recorded in the Courts of Heaven. Your word becomes active the second it escapes your lips. It will hit its mark like a torpedo. *Pey Final* shows you will be responsible for the glory or for the damage.
>
> *Y.A. Butler*

Standing before an open field, a rumble vibrates the very core of my spirit. Beyond a vibration—it's the sound of thunder from deep within. Each crack of the thunder explodes louder still until the sound can no longer be contained. The grass of the field stands to attention, the rocks turn their gaze, the mountains arrange, leaning in to the sound they recognize. With a gentle breeze blowing from behind to carry the words spoken—even the leaves on the trees rustle in silence. All of creation begins to groan not only at the revelation of the words being spoken, but the revelation of a son. This is *Pey Final*.

Daniel Cook

TSADE

MODERN

EARLY	MIDDLE	LATE

18

T'sade is the side. It is a journey of the righteous and staying on the path. It is on the hunt, on the chase. It is charity as a vital act of justice.

> Side: The early ancient Semitic/Hebrew of Tsade (ᚻ) some say represents a man on his side, others say a trail. The Hebrew word *tsad* (צַד) means *side* (Strong's H6654).

> Journey of the righteous; staying on the path: A trail is meant for a journey. The Hebrew word *tsad·dēk'* (צַדִּיק) means *righteous* (Strong's H6662). Tsade reminds us a righteous man seeks out the path Yahweh has for him and stays on it.

> To hunt, chase (צוּד) *tzuwd*: The root word for Tsade is the Hebrew *tsüd* (צוּד) which means *to hunt* (Strong's H6679). Tsade reminds us that we need to hunt for, or search out, the mysteries Yahweh has for us.

> Charity as a vital act of justice: The Hebrew word *tsed·ä·kä'* (צְדָקָה) means *justice* and *righteousness* (Strong's H6666). It also signifies charity. Charity should be vital act of justice.

Elizabeth R. Corley

Our seats or thrones in our throne rooms are called mercy seats. I hear a warning from Eber passionately saying to always keep our great letter *Tsade* with us in these seats. Tsade represents the righteous, humbled man who always gives honor and praise to Yahweh.

Tsade, we humbly and thankfully keep you with us in our throne. We ask that we may see all of your sides and dimensions of righteousness as we remain seated in this holy place. Thank you, Tsade.

Aaron Smith

⸺Ⴤ⸺

Tsade. I love that Tsade speaks of a journey and a path. It speaks of the righteous. Some examples of *tsadik*, or those on this path of righteousness who are significant to me include Zadok, Melechzadok, and last but not least, Adonizedek, the Lord of Righteousness or *YHWH TSADIK*. Our journey on this path of righteousness unfolds daily, if not momentarily, with discoveries of mysteries and glory. A wonderful scripture for meditation on Tsade is "This is what the LORD says: 'ask for the ancient paths, ask where the good way is, and walk in it, and you will find rest for your souls'" (Jer. 6:16 NIV).

Teresa Bowen

⸺Ⴤ⸺

Tsade is the transforming power of righteousness. He demonstrates to me the desire of a justified heart. He is hungry for justice and judgment. He longs to see all things redeemed. He gets involved with others not to be condescending, but to lead in the path as the example in uprightness. His character is settled. He will not compromise.

Y.A. Butler

⸺Ⴤ⸺

Tzade is the righteous one. I have long understood this letter largely by the way it looks. The letter looks like one who is on their knees, face toward heaven and hands in the air. It is a perfect picture of our communion with Yahweh.

This communion brings about the meaning of the word "righteous one." As of late, I have begun to see this letter in a new way. Tzade also looks like the letter Nun with a Yod placed on his shoulders.

Yod is a faithful son, who not only has the all-spark of creation inside—the little dot that contains much—but he has also chosen to carry that seed (*yod*) to completion. Why, I wonder? This faithful, righteous son has seen the completion from the beginning and has chosen to carry it.

> For unto us a Child is born, Unto us a Son is given; And the government will be upon His shoulder. And His name will be called Wonderful, Counselor, Mighty God, Everlasting Father, Prince of Peace. Of the increase of His government and peace There will be no end, Upon the throne of David and over His kingdom, To order it and establish it with judgment and justice From that time forward, even forever. The zeal of the LORD of hosts will perform this (Isa. 9:6-7).

Daniel Cook

ץ

TSADE FINAL

Tsade Final stands with arms lifted upward in praise.

Arms lifted upward in praise: Tsade Final (ץ) is written as a Nun Final (ן) with an ascending Yud. It looks like a righteous son with arms raised upward in victory and praise, saying, "According to thy name, O God, so is thy praise unto the ends of the earth: thy right hand is full of righteousness" (Psalm 48:10).

Elizabeth R. Corley

Tsade, the Priest:

On earth you continuously gaze at the Father with eyes from the four different faces of Lion, Ox, Eagle, and Man. From heaven, you speak to the earth from the four faces of Cherub, Lion, Eagle, and Man. You ascend and descend between Heaven and earth, loving Justice and bringing Mercy. *Tsade Final* is a priest of righteousness.

Y.A. Butler

So, the journey began... With the vision of the completed work squarely on my shoulders, and Holy Ghost as my guide, I began to search, listen, and watch. So often the path was dark and many times the next step was a leap of faith. I could not tell if there was firm ground, or a pit. Yet deep within the root of what He had placed on my shoulders, I knew peace: peace I couldn't understand or explain.

I took one more step.

With each step, a light would shine brighter from within my heart. From there I could see that the deepest roots of what He had placed on my shoulders was intertwined as well. And each step brought the light to shine brighter still.

As the light became brighter and brighter, I looked and saw what He had placed on my shoulder: everything that I ever had need of, everything that He had made me to be, the supply for every work, the blessing of every sacrifice, the abundance of Heaven, the fullness of Himself, and the ability to complete what I had seen from the beginning was already there. All I needed was to access it.

This is *Tsade Final*.

Daniel Cook

QUPH

MODERN

EARLY   MIDDLE   LATE

*Q*uph is Yahweh's hand blessing, protecting, and circling us, raising us up from the depths to set us apart to be Holy.

> Yahweh's hand blessing, protecting, and circling us: The modern Hebrew Quph is written as a Kaf either touching (ק) or hovering (ק) over a Vav. Quph reminds us that Yahweh is our covering, our protection—He surrounds us.

> Raising us up from the depths: The modern Hebrew Quph is the lowest of the main letters. The Vav of Quph extends below the base line. Quph reminds us that Yahweh raises us up from the depths of bondage (Jer. 32:21).

> To set us apart to be Holy: The Hebrew *kä·dash'* (קָדַשׁ) means "holy, to consecrate, or to be set apart" (Strong's H6942). Yahweh calls us to be holy as He is holy:

>> For I am the LORD that bringeth you up out of the land of Egypt, to be your God: ye shall therefore be holy, for I am holy (Lev. 11:45).

>> *Elizabeth R. Corley*

ק

The nineteenth letter is *Quph*, and Eber says this letter is aligned perfectly with the number 19. Nineteen's personality is quiet by nature, but when she speaks, she connects that which had been disconnected. Quph is similar in character and nature in that when she speaks, it's about measurement. Until now, her methods of measurement were limited by the rotation of the earth around the sun.

When we entered Zion, Quph was enabled to speak of the dimensions of time and to begin to present a new way of time-keeping. Quph is ready to speak as we give place to her, as we honor time by the pattern she describes. She readily admits that she is only a part of the time path, but she honorably holds a key to the door of understanding time in this dimension of Up Here. She works well with The Spirit of Understanding and her color is likewise yellow. Let us honor Quph in our engaging Olam.

Aaron Smith

Quph is the sun on the horizon. It can be interpreted as the sun coming up or going down, depending on the time in this dimension. Quph's essence is holiness. From it, we get the word *kodesh*, holy. It is the only letter that descends below the line of the writing. So to me, Eber is revealing a dual function in Quph. Quph descends into the secret places, what we call night, to bring the holy and take us into mystery. It reaches up, ascending to holiness and perfection in what we call day and brings forth the revelation of glory.

Teresa Bowen

Quph is the taking of dominion of the "now." It is the realization that today is my day. Today I walk in righteousness. Today I set myself apart to walk in holiness. No longer am I bound to "maybe someday" thinking. Quph demonstrates the blessing of deleting wishful thinking by persevering in the present moment.

Y.A. Butler

Quph. "Imitate God, therefore, in everything you do, because you are his dear children" (Eph. 5:1). Quph is a place of process. The letter means "copy" and "sun on the horizon." As of late, Yahweh has been speaking to me regarding the completion from the Beginning. As I meditated on this, I began to realize how the completion of anything that man has brought into this earth first began with a thought. As we hear a word, or see a vision, or just simply think a thought, our mind sees the completion of that word, dream, or thought. We see the fullness from the very Beginning. As we continue meditating, a process to complete this thought is laid out. Do you remember the day you were saved…? Do you remember the words Yahweh has spoken over you…? Do you remember who you are, royalty of Yahweh…? I have always seen Quph as one standing before a mirror. The reflection is the completed work. The best part? The completion of His word in us is always exceedingly abundant above all we could ask or think. This is Quph.

Daniel Cook

RESH

ר

MODERN

EARLY	MIDDLE	LATE

20

*R*esh is the head, the beginning, the top, and means "to lead." It is to see around corners and to see the original intent.

> Head, beginning, top; to lead: The early ancient Semitic/ Hebrew of Resh (𐤓) is a head of man. The modern Hebrew Resh looks like the top of a head. The Hebrew word *rōshe* (רֹאשׁ) means "head, top, summit, chief, beginning" (Strong's H7218).

> To see around corners; see the original intent: The modern Hebrew Resh also looks like a Vav bending around a corner. It is man (ו) able to see around corners to see Yahweh's original, beginning intent.

> *Elizabeth R. Corley*

Eber declares that *Resh* has never been at home in the dimensions of war and death. Resh worked well with Ruach Kodesh to bring to pass this great age of peace. Resh is commissioned to be part of the verbiage in the courts that legally gives us rights to obtain the mind of Christ. Resh makes the sound to look to see what He will say to us, as we take advantage of our rights to look into the future to affect the now. Resh, you are amazing in that your heart is to reveal knowledge that was hidden for ages but now you are speaking. Resh, we recognize your color is indigo for you work well with The Spirit of Knowledge.

Aaron Smith

Resh is the head of time, the Olam, the origin, and/or original intent. The original intent is for man to live as a glorious light being with a higher consciousness in the image of Yahweh.

So, it makes sense that Quph comes before Resh in sequence. To return or "re-member" ourselves to our original intent, we must ascend to negotiate the image and then descend to live "on earth as it is in heaven." This in turn causes us to live at the higher state of being and to see around corners, to not only know future events, but to be the catalyst to create the future.

Teresa Bowen

Resh is one of the most powerful tools revealed. It is a guarded gate through which the Seven Spirits of the Lord can enter and teach. It is a mind not deceived by its own imaginations. It is a renewed mind. It's a humbled mind. This mind, united with the Holy Ghost, has access to divine secrets and mysteries. It is not bound to conformity. It dances through limitless possibilities and creates with desire.

Y.A. Butler

Resh is the head or beginning. Resh is one of four letters that are beginnings. Aleph (Yahweh)—the beginning from which all the letters are contained. Hey—the beginning of a word spoken to us, and the breath that gives life. Yod (Yahshua)—the beginning of all letters: every letter written begins with a dot, or Yod. Resh—the beginning of fulfillment and the action of authority. These four letters combine to make the word *ariyeh* (אריה), or lion. The Lion of the tribe of Judah, the beginning of our praise. The letters also combine to form the word *yirah* (יראה). *Yirah Yahweh* is the fear of the Lord. Proverbs 9:10 teaches that the beginning of wisdom *is* the fear of the Lord. Let's begin!

Daniel Cook

SHIN

MODERN

EARLY	MIDDLE	LATE

Shin is the tooth: it means sharp, press, to be pierced, to sharpen. It means to lay hold and not let go.

> Tooth; sharp, press, to be pierced, to sharpen: The early ancient Semitic/Hebrew of Shin (ᗰ) is a tooth. I think it looks more like a back molar than front teeth. The Hebrew word *shān* (שֵׁן) means *tooth* (Strong's H8127). It is from the root word *shä·nan'* (שָׁנַן) which means "sharpen, prick, to teach diligently" (Strong's H8150).

> To lay hold and not let go: As teeth are used to bite food, Shin reminds us we need to lay hold of the things of Yahweh and not let go of them (1 Tim. 6:12, 19).

Shin to me is three flames representing Yahweh יהוה, Yahshua יהושע, and Ruwach Kodesh רוח קדש; Who is The All-Sufficient God, *El Shaddai* אל שדי And the Prince of Peace, *Sar Shalom* שר-שלום.

Elizabeth R. Corley

Shin is one of the letters that has already been verbal for a while. He began to express to us his position as part of the divine name of *Yod Hey **Shin** Vav Hey*. The tetragrammaton of YHVH with Shin inserted in the middle of the four letters refers to Yahshua, but I believe Shin is also speaking of another dimension, specifically the unity spoken of in John chapter 17. John 17 speaks of all of us being inserted in the Name together. Eber speaks to me that Shin is the letter sealed and stamped into our hearts for the sake of us being identified in the realms of heaven and all creation. Shin is not only the flames of fire or the sharp teeth that hold onto the promises, but he also represents our crowns.

As the twenty-four elders cast their crowns before the throne (Rev. 4:10), we likewise identify with them that our crowns are in Him, our Messiah, Yahshua. Shin is our letter together shared with Yahshua. Shin is our witness from the letters that we are all one together in each other and in Him. You are amazing, Shin, and we rejoice together with you!

Aaron Smith

The Paleo Hebrew definition of *Shin* is *teeth*, which has never settled well in my spirit. The main reason is that when we insert Shin into the tetragrammaton, as *Yod Hey **Shin** Vav Hey*, to mean Yahweh and Yahshua, with the Shin representing Yahshua: well, calling Him *teeth* just does not sit well with me. But to know Eber's definition of Shin as the awe-spark of Yahweh, then YES! Yahshua is definitely that and dwells in us by His Spirit, so that we house this very awe-spark of Yahweh ourselves. The Shin is featured on the tefillin (a box worn on the forehead) of Orthodox Jewish men. A three-headed Shin faces people looking at the wearer and a four-headed Shin is on the back of the tefillin, concealed from view. The three-headed shin represents the world that is, as well as the three desert fathers, Abraham, Isaac, and Jacob. The four-headed shin represents the world to come, or that which is not seen presently, and the four desert mothers, Sarah, Rebecca, Leah, and Rachel. I find it fascinating to see the mother side of Yahweh in these desert mothers who bring to bear the world to come. Selah.

Teresa Bowen

Until I met *Shin* I never knew that peace could destroy chaos. I had believed it was the other way around, but peace is much stronger. Shin reminds me that my seat/position is secure. I need not fear loss. Peace is my location and my vocation. It's an eating or a taking in, and then it becomes a permanent part of who I am. I am complete. I lack nothing. Chaos may be around me, but I am not disturbed. Throughout the path of life, the fire of Shin is the lava bubble that burns all around the righteous. We consume and are consumed. We are purified and live in the all-consuming fire of Yahweh's heart.

Y.A. Butler

Shin is the place of action. Just as a tooth is used to consume the food being eaten, and fire consumes the fuel, so it is with Shin. Just as we hear the word of Yahweh, and allow that word to change us to become more like Him, so it is with Shin. Just as Yahweh sent His only Son, Yahshua, to bring forth many sons, so it is with Shin.

Daniel Cook

TAV

ת

MODERN

+	✕	ת
EARLY	MIDDLE	LATE

22

Tav is the mark and covenant. It represents *of*—when we are in covenant with Yahweh, we are *of* Him. It is considered the end letter. It is finishing to begin something new.

> Mark, covenant: The early ancient Semitic/Hebrew of Tav (+) is a mark. It almost looks like "X marks the spot." The Hebrew word *täv* (תָּו) means "a mark; by implication, a signature, a mark as a sign of exemption from judgement" (Strong's H8420). I think it looks more like a cross. Tav reminds us of the covenant Yahshua made possible through His death on the cross and His resurrection.

> *Of*, when in covenant with Yahweh, we are *of* Him: Tav can be used as a suffix meaning *of*. To be of something means you are part of it or you are with it. When we are in covenant with Yahweh, we are called the Sons of God, the children of God. We are in Him and He is in us. We are *of* Him.

> The end letter; finishing to begin something new: In modern Hebrew, Tav is the last letter, so it is considered the finishing letter. This finishing is not an end, but an opportunity to begin something new. As the mark of the finish leading to something new, it does not imply going around the same mountain again, but it impels us to build on the cycle, to move forward and up. As such, it is or becomes symbolic of a spiral ascending, pointing us to Ghah.

Elizabeth R. Corley

The finishing letter is *Tav*. I love Tav, as I do all of the letters, but I fit with him and understand him. He's the mark in the road or the point of finishing. You may be saying to yourself, wait a minute, we have another letter. You are correct, but our next letter, Ghah, is not the finishing letter. I'm thankful that Tav is not an end, but a finishing point. I've said it many times in the past couple of years, and I agree it's difficult to remember, but Yahweh is about finishing—not endings. Endings are the influence of Greek linear thinking. I sense Yahweh sighing every time I slip up and pronounce an ending when I should have pronounced a finishing. I believe Tav's ancient form as a cross is so appropriate. Yes, it is shaped just like the crosses that are worn as a mark of the crucifixion and symbolic of Christianity. The cross of Christ was definitely a mark of finishing—as He said while hanging from the cross: "It is finished." So I wonder, when He saw the cross, did He see a Tav, a finishing and a fulfilling, instead of a cross of death, an end? I'm confident He did. May the Tavs of our scrolls be not symbols of death, or endings of life, but our signs of eternal and everlasting life. Eber says that Tav will be very busy in this great place of Mt Zion. Tav encourages us to go into the depths with him that we may mark the paths for those to follow. He loves those of us who are pioneers, for we are not afraid to go down a path uncharted by man. We are drawn to discover Yahshua's markings on the walls and dimensional paths. May we always recognize and honor you, Tav.

Aaron Smith

Tav is the mark. This letter begins the word *tikkun*, meaning to rectify, redeem, or make whole; to return the sparks of the divine back to their heavenly source. *Tikkun Olam.*

The earth is marked by Yahweh to be made new. We are marked as sons of Yahweh to be the builders, the ones to bring about this redeeming and rebuilding (Isa. 61).

Teresa Bowen

Tav. Written in red on our scroll, Tav speaks: "IT… IS… FINISHED!" Selah.

Y.A. Butler

Tav is completion, fulfilment, and original intent. Our journey through the Hebrew letters always brings us to this place: "Today I call you son… Well done—you are My sons in whom I am well pleased." Tav is the mark of revelation that you have always been what you were always meant to be. את.

Daniel Cook

GHAH

Ghah means twisted. I believe Yahweh has a reason for folding Ghah into Ayin ע, so we would look, see, and search out the mysteries Yahweh has in Ghah. Here are only a few:

To me, Eber has revealed that Ghah is an ascending and descending letter. In writing Ghah, I must first spiral up—ascend to the presence of Yahweh—and then spiral down—descend with a shout of Yahweh's word.

One of the Hebrew words for spiral is Luwl (לוּל). The word is found in 1 Kings 6:8, which tells of Solomon building the Temple. A spiral staircase is taken to the Holy of Holies, to signify ascending to the presence of Yahweh. Some say Ghah also means dark. If we take the word Luwl (לוּל), spiral, and replace the letter Vav ו with Yud י, then the word becomes the Hebrew word for night, (לַיְל), Layil. In Genesis 1:5, we read, "And God called the light Day, and the darkness he called Night. And the evening and the morning were the first day."

In this verse, Yahweh called the darkness (choshek חֹשֶׁךְ) layil לַיְל or in English, night. Yahweh twisted day into night and night into day.

This twisting can also be seen in the tzitzit (צִיצָת) or tassels on the corners of a tallit (טלית) (prayer shawl). In Numbers 15:38, Yahweh commanded the Israelites to put fringes/tassels on the corners of their garments and put on a blue-violet thread upon the fringes. The Hebrew for this blue-violet is תְּכֵלֶת Tekhelet (pronounced tek·ā'·leth). Strong's states the dye for this color is from the cerulean mussel, a species thought to be lost. Various sources in Judaism describe the dye as being "black as midnight," "blue as the midday sky," and even purple. I believe Yahweh hid the letter Ghah in the color of Tekhelet, twisting night into day and day into night.

Many Jewish rabbis and scientists have attempted to find the source of the dye. In 1913, Rabbi Herzog proposed the dye could have been produced from secretions collected from Hexaplex trunculus, a sea snail species which lives in the Mediterranean Sea. This dye is initially dark purple, not quite the blue-violet color directed by Yahweh. So, Herzog's theory seemed to fall short. Yet, later in the 1980s, a scientist discovered that if the dye from Hexaplex trunculus is exposed to ultraviolet rays, like sunlight, a blue color is consistently produced. The dye goes from dark into sunlight to produce the blue as day.

The dye colors the threads used for tying the tzitzit (tassels). The tzitzit has four threads at each corner. The four threads are folded to make eight threads hanging from each corner, for a total of thirty-two threads hanging on a tallit. Each set of eight threads is tied with five knots. In between the knots, the blue thread is wrapped around the other threads. The number of times the blue thread is wrapped represents Yahweh's name. It may be wrapped 10-5-6-5, to represent the letters of His name, Yod Hey Vav Hey, יהוה. Or, it may be wrapped 7-8-11-13, to represent "Yahweh is one." 7 + 8 = 15, The number 15 is written in Hebrew as Yud-Hey הי the beginning of Yahweh's name. The rest of Yahweh's name is Vav-Hey which is 6 and 5. 6 + 5 = 11. The number 13 represents the Hebrew word for one, *echad* (אחד). Aleph 1 + Chet 8 + Dalet 4 = 13.

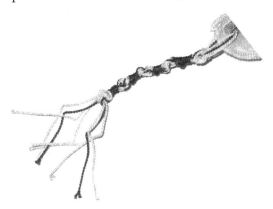

The wrapping of the thread looks like a spiral. It is Yahweh's name represented by the letter Ghah. Yahweh uses Ghah to remind us to ascend.

Elizabeth R. Corley

The last letter of the twenty-three letters is our friend, *Ghah*. While the Hebrews were in Babylonian captivity, Ghah was joined with Ayin to create the letter Ghayin, which was used for a time while the Hebrews were in captivity. It's fascinating to me that such a powerful letter had to be hidden from their captors. Eber reveals that Ghah has been associated as wicked in the sense of being twisted, but that has been its disguise. When Yahweh began to encourage me to write decrees, He awakened me to the letter Ghah. When I began to engage with Ghah, He pointed to the letter Ayin. Then both letters revealed to me twelve more letters that have been hidden until we entered the ages of peace. These letters point to the words *layil* and *luwl*. These words describe the spiraling staircase that lead to a deep dark place of Yahweh, called *Choshek*. *Choshek* is where the hidden treasures are to be found by the family of God and redeemed to purpose. We must commune with the Spirit of Understanding in order to fully engage with this amazing place.

When I engage these twelve letters, their expressions are dimensional. When they finish speaking, they send their messages back through Ayin, then through the last step of Ghah before they can release a tangible word. Ghah is the path into the mysteries, the path out, and the path back into this world. We cannot change heaven and earth without his door being opened and in some cases, closed.

Eber says that Ghah is the written and spoken path to Olam. Thank you, Ghah.

Aaron Smith

Ghah is the mystery letter that has been called out of darkness into marvelous light. It is the spiral staircase that leads to the hidden, secret places. Note the plural use of *places*: these are places yet unseen and still unknown. Ghah has been hidden in the Ayin, the eye. If the eye hooks into Ghah, then revelation that's been hidden for generations will be revealed to the one willing to look into Ghah. As Isaiah said, "Here I am Lord, send me." So I will go into the places of mystery not yet known to man and bring the apocalypse to the praise of His Glory.

Teresa Bowen

Ghah is the secret stair case. It makes perfect sense to me that Ghah has been hidden for so long. It was hidden in plain sight... waiting... waiting... for us. Ghah was hidden in Ayin, which is perception. Yahshua often said, "He who has ears to hear, let him hear." As for Ghah, I say, "He who has eyes to see, let him perceive!" So, hidden there among the mysteries and secrets of the universe, an ancient creature is finally discovered! It's the ladder of ascending and descending between heaven and earth. To me, Ghah is the chord of the *Mahanaim*. Ghah teaches us how to dance between the worlds; how to start where we have finished and begin again... ever increasing, ever living in the Olam.

Y.A. Butler

Ghah is the divine dance of ever increasing glory and the perfection of Our love. It is the spiralling of the two already as One discovering the treasure of the depths of who We are. I paraphrase John 17:21: "Father, that they may be one, as You and I are One... We are One."

Daniel Cook

BONUS SECTION ON GHAH

Ghah no longer exists in modern Hebrew. It was absorbed into the sixteenth letter of the Hebrew Aleph-Beyt, Ayin. Some consider Ghah to be the twenty-third letter, following Tav. The positional difference between Ayin (at letter 16) and Ghah (at letter 23) is seven. The formation of the letter suggests a rope of twisted fibers and therefore represents the concept of twist, twisted, or twisting (See Table 1 for Hebrew words with the meaning *twist*).

Ghah is found on the Wadi El-Hol inscriptions, located in Egypt, dated 2000 B.C. Jeff A. Benner suggests that Ghah was folded into Ayin, because several words which contain the letter Ayin have dual meanings.[5] Duality of meaning is rare in Hebrew. When such duality occurs, it suggests the word in question was originally two different words which later merged. (See Table 2, Words with Dual Meanings, for examples.) Some find that the word Ghah appears to represent dark or wicked concepts, and therefore conclude that Ghah represents darkness and wickedness. Perhaps because the Ghah-words were dark and wicked, Ghah had to be absorbed into Ayin.

However, let's consider the possibility that Yahweh purposefully folded Ghah into Ayin, which represents the eye, as a mystery to be searched out at the right time. Proverbs 25:2 states, "It is the glory of God to conceal a thing: but the honour of kings is to search out a matter."

---

5   Benner, Jeff A. "The Ancient Hebrew Alphabet - Ghayin." Ancient Hebrew Research Center. Accessed February 20, 2018. http://www.ancient-hebrew.org/alphabet_letters_ghayin.html.

In this verse, the Hebrew word translated as *thing* and *matter* is dä·vä’ (דָּבָר), which is also the word for *word*. The Hebrew for *conceal* is sä·thar’ (סָתַר), which is also the word for *hide* or *secret*. We can conclude, then, that Yahweh has secret words for us to search out.

Consider that Ghah looks something like a spiral staircase, ascending and descending. The word lül (לוּל) means spiral step; winding stairs (Strong's H3883), and it is found in 1 Kings 6:8. "The door for the middle chamber was in the right side of the house: and they went up with *winding stairs* into the middle chamber, and out of the middle into the third". This is the spiral staircase in Solomon's Temple leading to the Holy of Holies.

By replacing the letter Vav in lül (לוּל) with a Yud, the word becomes lah’·yil (לַיִל), which means twist (away of light); night (Strong's H3915). Lah’·yil (לַיִל) is found in Genesis 1:5—"And God called the light Day, and the darkness he called Night. And the evening and the morning were the first day." The Hebrew word translated *darkness* is khō·shek’ (חֹשֶׁךְ). So, Yahweh called the darkness (khō·shek’) night (lah’·yil), which represents the twisting of light, or day, into night. The night, lah’·yil, reminds us of lül, the spiral steps that lead to the Holy of Holies.

Now consider Ghah also means a rope of twisted fibers. The four corners of a Tallit, the Hebrew prayer shawl, have threads of twisted fibers. Deuteronomy 22:12 states, "Thou shalt make thee fringes upon the four quarters of thy vesture, wherewith thou coverest thyself."

The Hebrew word translated *fringes* is ghed·ēl’ (גְּדִל), meaning twisted threads, tassels or festoons. It is from the primitive root word gä·dal’ (גָּבַל), meaning to twist, to grow, increase, lift up or promote. The fringes on the corners of the Israelite's garments are tied to represent Yahweh's name.

We can conclude that Yahweh hid Ghah in the fringe that represents His name. Just like His name has been hidden and revealed, Ghah, once hidden, is now being revealed.

Elizabeth R. Corley

Hebrew Words with the Meaning *Twist* or *Twisted*

אוּל	H193	Pronunciation: ül Definition: from an unused root meaning to **twist**, i.e. (by implication) be strong; the body (as being rolled together); also powerful:—mighty, strength. Translation: mighty, strength
גָּבַל	H1379	Pronunciation: gä·val' Definition: a primitive root; also as a denominative from H1366 properly, to **twist as a rope**; to bound (as by a line):—be border, set (bounds about). Translation: border, set bounds, set
גְּבוּל	H1366	Pronunciation: ghev·ül' Definition: (shortened) from H1379; properly, a cord (as **twisted**), i.e. (by implication) a boundary; by extension the territory inclosed:—border, bound, coast, × great, landmark, limit, quarter, space. Translation: border, coast, bound, landmark, space, limit, quarters,
גַּבְלֻת	H1383	Pronunciation: gav·lüth' Definition: from H1379; a **twisted** chain or lace:—end. Translation: the ends
חֶבֶל	H2256	Pronunciation: kheh'·vel Definition: from H2254; a rope (**as twisted**), especially a measuring line; by implication, a district or inheritance (as measured); or a noose (as of cords); figuratively, a company (as if tied together); a throe (especially of parturition); also ruin:—band, coast, company, cord, country, destruction, line, lot, pain, pang, portion, region, rope, snare, sorrow, tackling. Translation: sorrows, cord, line, coast, portion, region, lot, ropes, company, pangs, hands, country, destruction, pain, snare, tacklings

חוּל	H2342	Pronunciation: khül Definition: a primitive root; properly, **to twist** or whirl (in a circular or spiral manner), i.e. (specifically) to dance, to writhe in pain (especially of parturition) or fear; figuratively, to wait, to pervert:—bear, (make to) bring forth, (make to) calve, dance, drive away, fall grievously (with pain), fear, form, great, grieve, (be) grievous, hope, look, make, be in pain, be much (sore) pained, rest, shake, shapen, (be) sorrow(-ful), stay, tarry, travail (with pain), tremble, trust, wait carefully (patiently), be wounded. Translation: pain, formed, bring forth, pained, tremble, travail, dance, calve, grieved, grievous, wounded, shake

Compiled by Elizabeth R. Corley

Words with Dual Meanings

	Originally with Ayin (ע)	Originally with Ghah (غ)
יעל	**profit** H3276 – 1 Sam. 12:21	**goat** H3277 – I Sam. 24:2; H3278 – Jdg 4:17
עול	**infant** H5763 – Gen. 33:13; H5764 – Isa. 49:15	**wicked** H5765 – Psa. 71:4; H5766 – Lev. 19:15; H5767 – Job 18:21
עור	**skin** H5783 (naked) – Hab. 3:9 H5784 (chaff) – Dan. 2:25 H5785 – Gen. 3:21	**blind** H5782 (awaken) – Deu. 32:11 H5786 – Exodus 23:8 H5787 – Exodus 4:11
עיף	**weary** H5888 – Jeremiah 4:31 H5889 – Gen. 25:29	**darkness** H5774 (fly) – Gen. 1:20 עוף H5890 (femine form) – Job 10:22 H5891 (gloomy) – Gen. 25:4
עיר	**colt** H5894 (watcher) – Dan. 4:13 H5895 – Gen. 32:15	**city** H5892 – Gen. 4:7 H5893 – I Chron. 7:12
ענה	**heed** H6031(afflict, humble) – Gen. 15:13	**answer** H6030 – Gen. 18:27 H6032 – Dan. 2:5 H6033 (poor) – Dan. 4:27 H6034 – Gen. 36:2
ערב	**weave** H6148 (pledge) – Gen. 43:9 H6149 (agreeable) – Psalm 104:34 H6151 (mix) – Dan. 2:41 H6152 (Arabia) - 1 Kings 10:15 H6154 (mixed) – Exodus 12:38	**dark** H6150 – Judge 19:9 H6153 – Gen. 1:5

	Originally with Ayin (ע)	Originally with Ghah (ﻍ)
ערם	**naked** H6192 (pile up) – Exodus 15:8	**crafty** H6191 – I Sam. 23:22 H6193 – Job 5:13
ערף	**neck** H6202 (break neck) – Exodus 13:13 H6203 – Gen. 49:8	**rain** H6201 (drop down) – Deut. 32:2
רע	**friend** H7453 – Gen.11:3; H7454(thought) – Psa. 139:2	**bad** H7451 – Gen. 2:9; H7452 – Exo. 32:17; H7455 – Gen. 41:19
רעה	**shepherd** H7462 – Gen. 4:2 H7463 (friend) – 2 Sam. 15:37 H7464 (female companion) – Judges 11:37	**break** H7465 – Prov. 25:19
שער	**hair** H8176 (think) – Prov. 23:7 H8177 – Dan. 3:27 H8179 (gate/heaven) - Gen. 19:1 H8180 (unit of measure) – Gen. 26:12 H8181 – Gen. 25:25	**storm** H8175 – Deut. 32:17 H8178 – Job 18:20 H8182 (vile) – Jer. 29:17

Compiled by Elizabeth R. Corley

CONCLUSION

Congratulations: I commend you for engaging Eber and the language of original intent. Engaging Eber will exponentially thrust you through dimensional doors and gates, opening mysteries that have been held for you for ages.

With *Friends of Eber* added to your library, you will find your word studies enhanced. You won't have to accept at face value the standard definitions you find in *Strong's*. You will be able to look into the meanings of each of the original Hebrew letters that make up the words. Applying the meanings of the letters will allow you to uncover the depth of a word's meaning.

I encourage you to find your Eber name. Your Eber name is made up of the living letters you've learned. It is the name Yahweh calls you, that defines you, that reveals who you are in Him. Find your name by getting the six Hebrew letters that speak to you most, or that seem to resonate with your spirit. My Eber name is Vav, Shin, Tsadi, Yud, Beit, Gimmel, or ושציבג, pronounced *Ashtssyoobegah*. It's ok to laugh here—we all do at how our Eber names sound. My name means *I am a secured peg connecting heaven and earth, burning with the awe-spark of Yahweh's fire that connects me to the ages to come where the righteous will traverse the universes in Yahweh's house with the running supply of treasure to do exceedingly abundantly above all that I could ask or think.*

Now it's your turn. Pick your six letters, put the sounds together, and look up their meanings. Write it all down and keep it before you.

Use this resource daily to find your Eber meanings of words that you read in your Bible. You will be blessed by the depth of our Father Yahweh's love in His original language.

Shalom,

Ashtssyoobegah

ושציבג

Teresa Bowen

Made in the USA
Columbia, SC
21 April 2022